New Agent Guide to a Successful 1st year in Real Estate

What you need to do when you get your license

By Adriel Roman

This Book Is dedicated to Heather Jo Burke, Zane and Cy Roman. #MyWhy!

Table of Contents

Preface

Introduction: My Story

First Thing: Pay Up

Second Thing: Time to Make an Important Decision

Third Thing: Make Your List

Fourth Thing: Socialize

Fifth Thing: Get Where You Can Be Seen

Sixth Thing: Sites and CRM

Seventh Thing: Start Your Routine

Eight Thing: Take Classes

Ninth Thing: Read Lots of Books & Listen to Audio Books

A Few More Things

Forward

I'm proud of my friend Adriel.

With this book he created something that is missing from the marketplace. There are 1000's of books on real estate strategies and achieving massive success in real estate. These books are typically aimed at real estate professionals trying to take their business to the next level.

In contrast, Adriel focuses on the soon to be new agent. He constructs a "How To" guide on the beginning steps of becoming a real estate agent. As with any successful business, a strong foundation is imperative.

As someone who has decided on pursuing real estate for a career, you are immediately presented with so many options that it can often cause paralysis.

Where do I hang my License?

What should I look for in a Brokerage?

How should I generate lead prospects?

Who should I ask for help?

How do I let my sphere know I'm a licensed real estate agent?

Who should I partner with?

Should I go on my own or join a team?

Etc., etc., etc.

With so many questions and opinions, it's important to block out the noise and get advice from someone that is not looking to profit off your decisions. Adriel's been there and done that and his advice is meant to guide you in constructing a real estate career that is right for you.

There is a great story on how this book came to be. Adriel's wife, Heather, decided to leave her corporate job and try her luck at real estate. Adriel is a successful individual real estate agent and wanted to help her during this transition. While putting together a list of tasks for her to focus on, he realized that new agents are thrust into making a lot of decisions that they are not prepared for. He came from a place of the heart to help his wife and other new agents avoid going through so much trial and error at the beginning of their career.

What you get with Adriel's book is an easy to read guide on starting your real estate career and setting yourself up for a long term career that is fulfilling, profitable, and allows you to focus on what's most important to you. For Adriel, that is family and community.

My favorite piece of Adriel's work is his advice to stay true to yourself. It's very easy to compare and judge yourself against other real estate agents and people in general. This can often lead one into being something they're not and also cause feelings of inadequacy and jealousy. What you value and what's important to you are very different than other agents. Don't get caught up in the comparison game.

Be true to yourself and you will attract people that value you for you.

Construct a career that works for you.

Adriel, awesome job buddy. I thoroughly enjoyed your book and the value it provides someone starting their career in real estate.

Reggie Green

Team Leader of Team Green

Branch Manager at Fairway Independent Mortgage

Preface

At the time of this writing I am completing my 6th year as a Real Estate Agent. The last 3 years I have been able to make a consistent 6 figures as an agent. The first 3 years I wasn't even close to six figures, which is part of the reason why I wrote this book.

My wife recently decided to leave her job in the healthcare industry. She had been spent the last 10 years plus with this company. She was there as they nearly imploded a few years ago and was an integral part of why they were able to turn it around and open enough offices to double in size a few years later. She was good at her job, respected by the owners and her co-workers loved her. But, she was not happy there anymore. She was struggling with the directions and decisions made by the newly hired upper management. Going to work became tougher, the environment was becoming toxic, employees were quitting or being fired on a weekly basis and it was killing her little by little every day she was there.

My wife told me she was considering going to Real Estate school and getting her license. She wasn't sure if she wanted to do what I did as a sales agent. She thought maybe she would get into property management or new construction homes sales, since there are so many new homes being built all around us.

Really??? I didn't understand.

Why become a real estate agent??? And, not be a sales agent??? I was confused, nervous, curious and anxious. I wondered what impression I had left on my wife regarding my career as a real estate agent?

When I started as an agent I would stress my wife out because I told her about how all my deals went. Why would she be interested in being an agent now? She knew of my failed attempts of building a team, twice! How the first was doomed from the start because I didn't choose a partner who shared the same vision I had for the team. And, the second was what I can only describe as a swift stabbing to the back, with a smile, immediately after having a record month together.

My wife and I spoke at lengths about how the average annual earning for a real estate agent is $45,000, which isn't horrible, but not too exciting either. She knew most agents only close 3 to 4 deals a year and make less than $35,000 a year. She knew my first few years were better than those numbers, and that they were exponentially better in my last 3 years. Maybe this was partly why she was considering becoming an agent.

I had so many crazy experiences in my first year as a real estate agent. My wife knew that I would constantly call up my broker and he was always bewildered by the questions I had or surprised by the latest situation I was in with my clients. I told her how my first Broker asked why I couldn't ever get any "easy" sales? To which I developed a response of, "I don't do easy!"

Talk about jinxing myself! With that mentality of course nothing was easy.

I know my wife was aware of the roller coaster ride that my income mimicked in the first couple of years I was an agent. Well, maybe not exactly a rollercoaster and more like a slalom. A very steep slalom, with many, many flags. I made more money than I had made at any job since the recession of 2008 but suffered the "peaks and valleys" so many agents experience. We would be eating out every night of the week for a month, then followed by eating ramen noodles the next month.

I still couldn't understand why I was so nervous and worried about her wanting to be a real estate agent. Maybe I was overreacting. I felt as if I needed to make sure she didn't go through what I did in my first few years. I wanted to get her as much info as possible to help her not make the mistakes I made or waste time trying to figure it out.

I do LOVE being a Real Estate Agent. I've made good friends and met some interesting people. I do make good money, now. My family goes on regular vacations when kids have their Spring, Summer, Fall and Winter school breaks. My business is 100% repeat clients and referrals now. I turn down business if I do not feel I will be comfortable working for someone. I have control over my business now.

But, that wasn't always the case….

So, I panicked. I could not let her go through the hardships I suffered my first few years. I needed to make sure she knew what to do once she got done with school and passed her tests. I searched for books she could read to get her ready, but I couldn't find one. This is the main reason why I wrote this book!

When I passed my test and got my license, I was excited for about 30 minutes. Then, came all the questions. What do I do now? Who do I need to call? What comes next? Who can help me?

Even my real estate school was no help with this. They just told me to find myself a brokerage and ask them there.

Yes, some brokerages will get you training and walk you through the first steps. But you might need to pay them first to join! Or, at least, decide to hang your license with them first. Which is what I did. And, I was lucky! The Broker I chose ran a small brokerage with less than 20 Agents. So, spending the time with me was worth it to him. Plus, I think he knew I was hungry. So, he was willing to put up with me in order to get me going quickly.

From the time I passed my test, to the day I hung my license with my broker 30 days had passed. Then it was another week of training on our systems before I received my first leads.

When I got started in real estate I felt lost, insecure and clueless. My first Broker called me #2. Not because I was his #2 producer but because, after his wife, I was the one who called him the most, so I was number 2 in his phone. I called him about everything, including how to use the Supra Key to open the lockbox and how to put the key back into the lockbox afterwards, at my first showing.

Some brokerages will assign a new agent a mentor or coach. They will usually ask for 30%-40% of your first 3-5 deals. But, I couldn't afford to lose that much of my commission after my split with my Broker. So, I went at it alone, though on a team.

What could I do? Well, I bought a bunch of books written by real estate agents. All the books out were about how to sell, and how to negotiate or listing presentations. Nothing on how to get started so I could get to selling. This didn't make sense to me. I felt all alone!

My hope is that this book will guide new agents through those crucial first steps. Hopefully, you will be less stressed, make better progress than I did in your first month and are able to execute with momentum to get your new career humming along.

None of this is difficult.

All of it is necessary.

I kept this book as short as possible without sacrificing any necessary details. It is compiled of the important things to do, preferably in the first 2 weeks, or, at the very least, in your first

30 days. Also included are tips on how to get yourself ready for the business. Things you can start on now so when your business ramps up you're ready to go. I believe that I ranked them in order of importance. So you can start showing homes and taking listings ASAP!

Oh, and congratulations! Great job at getting your license!

Introduction: My Story

I know I was very lucky when I first became a real estate agent! After I got licensed, I found a Broker who was very successful, into personal development and focused his time perfecting the marketing campaigns he had in place. This was such a blessing because things moved so quickly in that first year. I just didn't know how much those two things would impact my business.

Because of the marketing and systems my Broker had in place I was able to close three deals in my first three months! And, in the following calendar year, I closed twenty-four transactions. All from my Brokers online lead generation and not one from my personal sphere of influence.

Not too bad!

The down side to this was that since I had chosen to work for a Boutique Brokerage and I had joined his team, I was lucky to get 35%-50% of the commission checks on all those transactions I worked on.

Yes, I was giving up 50%-65% of my hard-earned commission to my Broker, AND, all contracts I wrote where in HIS name! (This is how those agents who claim they do 200-400 personal transactions a year do it) So, I did not even get any recognition for my work. But, at the time, I didn't care! I was a real estate agent! To me getting 50% of something was better than 100% of nothing. At least that is how he sold me on the split.

I stayed with that Broker for 2 ½ years! And, I learned some things that to this day I still use. I can't say that I regret that decision. But, when I think about the money I left "on the table", it drives me nuts.

It took for my first broker to change his business model for me to leave his team. His new model would have paid me, and other team members, a salary (about $18,000 a year) and a lesser split (about 5%) of the total commission. This just wasn't going to work for me. I am still not sure how he grew his team with this model. But, he did.

I consider myself to be loyal, so, at first, I tried another team in the brokerage, but that was not any better. How could it have been! So, I left and went over to 2 different 100% Commission Brokerages before finding my home with My Home Group. Again, I learned the hard way and I benefited from the experiences.

When I was with my first broker he provided the leads, website, Customer Relations Manager, transaction coordinator and even had people calling to schedule appointments, if I wanted. Now, being a solo agent, I had to do this myself and learn the systems to put in place for myself. And, this wasn't cheap!

Suddenly, I found myself spending more than $5,000 a month just to get leads. Plus, paying for the CRM and website which was another $500-$1000 monthly. On top of that was another $300 per close to a transaction coordinator. Talk about stress!

On my own I had to set up my autoresponders for incoming leads, create all the email drip campaigns, place ads on 5-10 different sites, make calls, upload paperwork and still find time to show homes.

My wife was still working full time, so along with my new responsibilities, I had to get my boys to school, daycare and doctors' appointments. Also, the oldest of my boys was diagnosed with ASD, Autism Spectrum Disorder, so we had therapies 4 times a week. I was constantly running around and overwhelmed.

So when my wife decided she wanted to get licensed, I felt that I needed to provide an outline for her so she could get selling as soon as possible and not feel overwhelmed, waste any time or repeat any of the mistakes I made.

I started writing up a game plan for her. I had trained in the Buffinin Peak Producer system and wanted to use that as our business model, so we would operate working our sphere of influence and by referral only. But, there was nothing in place that I could refer her to for the critical first few steps once she passed the tests and had her real estate license.

This is where the idea to write this book was birthed.

What This Book Is Not

This book isn't going to give you the scripts you need when meeting a client. There are enough of those available. It isn't about your Listing Presentation. Or offer any sales techniques at all. Though I will mention, and recommend, working your sphere of influence and by referral.

I am not going to give you the best ad templates to run on Facebook. Or, how to engage on Twitter with your followers. Though you should know you need a Social Media presence, or you are toast in this business today.

I am not going to tell you how to dress, how to qualify your buyers, or suggest where is the best place to meet your clients for the first time is.

I may write those books later. Maybe!

This book is about those critical first few steps you should make immediately after getting your license. I want to make sure you maximize time and get yourself to the place where you are ready to start working in your business, showing homes, quickly.

... And, maybe also to get you to pick up the books I write on the subjects above when I put them out!

I Am A Little Different Than Most

Full disclosure, I am a Law of Attraction practitioner.

There! I said it! And, I am proud of it!

No, I am not going to tell you to ask, believe and receive then watch your dream clients come to you as you do nothing but pet your cat. That's not what LOA is really about, in spite of the translation by many lazy individuals.

I bring up being a Law of Attraction practitioner because this is what has dramatically changed my life and my career. By being able to clearly identify what I want my business to be like, I have become the person who attracts the type of clients I enjoy working with. Working in real estate isn't always easy, so you need to really like who you are working for or you will regret every minute of your career. You need to spend the time working on yourself and becoming the type of person who attracts the type of clients you want to work with.

I also bring this up because if something I write doesn't feel right to you, or you do not believe it will apply to you, then I don't want you to do it! Try doing it your way. Your way might be better! You have a better understanding of where you are and who you are. I want you to be true to yourself. You will find out if you are correct soon enough. You will have this book to refer to. I believe that being true to who you are comes before anything that you can learn from me in this book.

Being a Real Estate Agent has been the most fulfilling job I have had. But it has also been the most difficult. I have learned to appreciate the difficult times and learn form them. I have learned immensely about myself because of this work. I have learned that I can attract the kind clients I want to work with. But first, I needed to become the person who can attracted them.

I learned to understand there is a balance in life. I cannot be swayed in either direction, good or bad. Sometimes what seems to be a bad situation turns into the most amazing experience. And, at the same time, what seems to be a good thing could be not so good.

My first Broker always said, "nothing is ever as good, or, as bad, as it seems." Knowing that has helped me more times than I can count.

Knowing about the Law of Attraction and how it works along with Personal Development principles for productivity, discipline and creating good habits have helped me to create an amazing life as a real estate agent.

I have helped many people buy their first home or moving here in search of better opportunities for their families. I have helped families that have moved to my state with a new job transfer, only have 30 days to find a home and move in, buy their home here only to have to sell it 6 months later because they found a better job opportunity elsewhere.

I have helped first time investors sell their first investment property, as well as a seasoned developer get back into the market after taking a beating back in 2008. I have helped couples recently married, couples going through divorce, families welcoming their first born and others who's relative had passed and needed to sell quickly.

You will have your own stories both good and bad. The better prepared you are, the more you develop your person, the more grateful you are for the opportunities to help others, the better off you will be in this career path. Getting paid is great! But, getting invited to house warming parties and having your clients talk about how awesome you were helping them purchase is priceless!

Yes, you are in sales! Yes, you are here to help in the purchase or sale of a home. But, please remember that in most cases you are helping someone with what might be the most important decision they ever make in their life.

Now let's get you ready to sell some homes!!!

First Thing: Pay Up

At this point you have paid for school and for your books. You paid to take your State and National tests and maybe to retest since more than 50% of us do not pass on the first take. Maybe you even paid for the test prep class.

Again, congratulations! You should be proud of yourself!

Now, guess what? You have even more things to pay for!

Department of Real Estate- If you haven't already, now you need to get yourself over to the State Department of Real Estate with your license application, proof of passed exam... and some cash! Every state varies on how much they charge, but typically it is between $100- $250.

Obviously, this isn't something new you've learned. But, it is very important to get this done as soon as possible. States vary on the processing of your license and how long it takes. It could be immediately done or take a couple of weeks.

If you're testing on a week day and you pass, I would personally recommend going straight to the department of real estate to get this taken care of. Get this out of the way as soon as possible.

… Because, right after the department of real estate you should go straight here next!

N.A.R. National Association of Realtors- Yes, I very much believe you need to join your Association. Sometimes, you will need to join more than 1, depending on where you are and where you want to practice. I know you can still work as a real estate agent without being a Realtor, but personally, you are better off being associated with the N.A.R.

I am fortunate that here in Arizona I can join ARMLS and work anywhere in the state. But, I do not have access to all the MLS info in other counties and my Supra Key doesn't work on lockboxes outside my specific location. It also helps when sending or receiving referrals, since we abide by the Code of Ethics you can be sure you'll receive better service on those you refer out and can count on collecting your referral fee.

No, it is not mandatory to join, but, if you are serious about your career, then I really think you should.

I have a friend who is a Broker and not a member of any associations here. He feels he doesn't need it because he only does property management. So, when he gets a new property to manage, guess who calls up for info??? Since he can't access the MLS and going by the info on Zillow is not dependable, he reaches out to me to get him the details on the homes.

I should probably start charging him, now that I think of it. But, he is a grumpy old man…

…My point is your doing yourself a disservice if you don't join.

Also, if you are not a Realtor, then you can't use the MLS to list your homes or see what is available for sale. Then, you are stuck depending on sites like Zillow and hoping they have the correct information you need. All that is unnecessary stress.

Misc.- Now you need to get all the tools of the trade. This includes, but is not limited to lockboxes, Supra Key or app, Business cards and Signs.

I put the business cards and signs on here because it will take time to get these made. So, if you do this now and it takes 3 weeks, you are still within the first 30 days from when you got your license. Obviously, you will need to choose a brokerage before spending money on creating your marketing materials first.

Some brokerages will offer you your first set of so many cards and maybe even one or two signs. It really depends on which direction you go with your decision on who to hang your license with. We will get into your options on brokerages and help in making that decision in the next chapter.

Since most of us start off showing homes to Buyers when we get our license, you will need the Supra Key or App on your phone. Most associations, if not all, have the agents use the electronic lockboxes so you will need these keys to get in. Mechanical or combination lockboxes are not too common anymore and are a liability for your listings. With the electronic lockboxes we as agents can track who was at your listing and when so we can provide that info to your sellers.

I strongly suggest either practicing opening a lockbox at your office or before your clients get there. You do not want to be at the door trying to figure this out in front of your clients. Or worse, you close the lockbox incorrectly and get the call from the angry Listing Agent because the next agent can't get in because of you.

Lockboxes are important if you plan on immediately getting listings. I didn't get my own lockbox until after being an agent for a few years. If I had a listing, I would rent the lockboxes at first. It gets pricey renting them. I suggest, if possible, buy 3. You can always be the one to rent them to those in your office if you are not using them.

There are other things you will need, like a smart phone, laptop and tablet. But if you do not have those already, then I am not sure how you made it this far.

I will get to other important tools like website and CRM later in the list.

Right now, all we want to do is get you up and running, fast!

Second Thing: Time to Make an Important Decision

Now it's time to make an important decision. One which will impact how you do in your first year more than anything else. It is time to decide who you will hang your license with!

Who will you add to your signature on your email?

Whose name will you have on your voice mailbox?

Who will you represent on your business cards?

This is the second most important thing you do when you become a real estate agent. The number one thing you do is third on my list of things to do. But, because we are trying to get you going as quick as possible this jumps into the number two spot on our list.

Because there is no "one size fits all" when it comes to choosing your brokerage, I can't help you with making this decision, but I will help you in trying to figure out what is the best fit for you based on what is important to you. There are a few types of brokerages and I will put them into 4 categories to make it easier for you to evaluate. This is an ever-growing industry and technology is changing the way brokerages operate constantly.

I believe the most important thing to remember is to surround yourself with people who are where you want to be. Try to associate with a brokerage who shares a similar belief system in their approach to client care. Also, you want to be in an environment of winners and not those doing the bare minimum to get by.

When I left my first broker I ended up at a brokerage near my home that offered 100% commission. They also offered me the opportunity to run the agent training program since I am a certified trainer for Buffini & Co Peak Producer. That offer to train the agents immediately turned into me being the Branch Manager for that office.

I was excited for the opportunity to run an office! I was excited to help all these agents! I was excited to help them recruit talent and grow the business!

But I didn't do my research on who was at this branch. And, it ended up being a small office full of agents who had spent many more years in the business than me, who wanted to continue getting by with as little effort as possible.

They never made any of the office meetings or training unless there was free food provided. Now, I like to eat as much as anybody. But, if a free meal is your motivation then you are in the wrong business.

You will have plenty of opportunities to eat in this business. Most of which will be on your dime. Get used to it!

I spent a little more than a year in this office of less than 30 agents. I personally did 40% of the transactions that office closed for that year. We closed 100 transactions that year as an office. Which is horrible! And I did 40 of those transactions myself!

Now, I understand many would love to be the "Rockstar" in their office. But, who do you turn to for support? Who do you use for motivation? I was miserable!

So, I went to a brokerage with nearly 2000 agents and some of the biggest and best agents and teams in the state of Arizona. Now, I am learning. Now, I am growing as an agent and a person. Now, I get the motivation of the monthly numbers of individual agents and teams that get posted to our private Facebook group every month. In August 2018 I cracked the top 20 solos agents list in our brokerage for the first time.

Now, I am making more money while working less hours and able to enjoy more time with family!

In school they will have Brokers come in and give you their pitch. Some will even say to start interviewing before you get your license. In my experience it was a waste of time.

I interviewed before having my license and though that I knew for sure who I was going to hang my license with. Then, within a month, that brokerage decided to merge with another and redo their whole business model. I didn't like the new location, partners or how the whole "vibe" of the office was now so I didn't join them. (Yes, I said "vibe")

So how do you decide which brokerage? Or, what type?

Well, let's get into the types of brokerages first to help narrow the field a bit.

Big Name Brokerages – These are the Keller Williams and ReMax's among many. Where you live might have Century 21 dominating the market. It all really varies.

Here, where I live in Arizona, there is a huge presence by ReMax. Since ReMax has a strong presence in Canada, I think something like 60% of the market there, and we get a ton of business from Canadian "Snow Birds" in the fall through Spring, they tend to gravitate towards a name brand they're familiar with.

Since people do feel more comfortable with brands they are familiar with, this may help get your business going if you're new to the industry.

Most of these brokerages have name brand familiarity, they have a history and can point to an agent or team that has really brought value to the name, like Keller Williams and Gary Keller.

They often will sell new agents on the training that they provide to new agents. Which I can't argue against. I almost joined KW because of this. They had a sweet back office with tons of training info and videos. I was impressed, for a bit.

The downside, in my opinion, is that with the number of agents signing up with these brokerages, because they can relate to the name branding effect on potential clients, how do you get the quality time you need from the Broker, coaches and Mentors they have in place. I have never been with one but do know they have the lowest retention rates in the industry generally. Especially because of the wave of new and innovative brokerages that leverage technology now.

Dinosaurs were big, scary and dominated the planet for many years. But, most were slow, blind and not able to adapt to changing environments. Hence, no more dinosaurs to worry about anymore!

I understand that you might get lucky and get a great Broker who has his system dialed in and ready to get you rocking in your first year. But the truth is most agents will leave their first brokerage, especially the big named ones, within the first year. You can really sabotage your business with a move like that! This is what I hope to help you avoid more than anything.

My other concern with these brokerages is the fees and commission splits associated with carrying their name. Branding is expensive! Carrying the name will cost you!

I am not up to date with who is charging what today. All I can tell you is that I once interviewed at one of these brokerages, which I won't name (rhymes with tree fax) and it was $500 a month to hang my license with them and the best they could do is offer me an 80/20 split.

You just got done spending some money to get your license, join an association, get your lockbox and Supra Key. Now you're expected to put up more money up front just to get your business going. Do you really want to add to the expenses, before you start making money?

That is a decision only you can make.

You might feel like the name and recognition outweighs the fees. Maybe you are self-motivated, a quick learner and don't need as much attention from the Broker and Coaches.

There is a reason they keep attracting agents. Maybe it's exactly what you need.

Maybe.

But before you make a decision let's see what else is out there.

Boutique Brokerages – These are typically smaller brokerages started by an agent with a team at a big name brokerage that decides to test their hand because of the success they've achieved.

They usually have a niche or unique selling proposition that they push out to attract attention. Maybe you've seen the "Flat Fee" brokerages or "If I don't sell your home in (Fill in the blank) then I will buy it myself".

This is the route I chose when I started as an agent. And, I chose the guys that will "buy your home" if they can't sell it.

They provided a ton of training and not only real estate specific. We did a lot of personal development, which was awesome!

Most of these brokers and owners are really into personal development and understand the value of marketing so they try to keep up with the latest marketing trends. They highlight the importance of health, routines and optimizing your daily schedule.

Since they usually do not have the deep pockets of the bigger names, they get creative with the marketing and training. They spend time with you on social media marketing, are up to date on the latest technology available to agents and stress the importance of your "List".

They invest in you as an agent because you directly affect their bottom line more than you will at a bigger brokerage. Which is great! But, could also be a problem, if they feel you're not "pulling your weight", or, if they are having a bad day.

I will admit that most of what I learned and still apply to my business came from my experience in a boutique brokerage. The scripts, the time blocking what is important and setting alarms for myself were all critical to my success.

But, these boutique brokerages are not all created equally! You really need to do your research on who is running the show and what type of numbers are they doing!

My reason for leaving my Boutique Brokerage had to do with the commission split. I didn't mind it much at first because I was making better money than I had ever to that point in my life. But when I finally evaluated the time I spent working versus the amount of my commission I got to take home, then it just didn't make sense.

When I started in real estate, I did not have a "List" or much of a Sphere of Influence, since I was somewhat new to Arizona. So, I accepted a 50/50 split for the buyer leads that I got to close escrow on. But the contracts were written in the Brokers name. So, the first 32 sales I made have his name on it, and I can't get them back.

If they set an appointment for me with a buyer, then I was down to 35/65 split. I am happy I only did a couple of these.

The experience was priceless, and I learned a lot. 27 transactions in my first 15 months wasn't bad. But they kept pushing for more. They challenged me to get to 50 transactions in a year.

But, I had started my family and needed to be available more nights and weekends. Not, work more or longer days.

I guess I got lucky that my Broker got greedy, um, I mean… "changed his business model". It allowed me to leave. Because it woke me up to how fragile a situation it was there.

You will find many blessings in this business that are disguised as bad news, or hard times. Embrace them! Learn from them!

So, my next move was to try the next type of brokerage on the list.

100% Brokerage- I ended up bouncing to a couple of these 100% Brokerages when I left my first broker. These are not as big as the big name brokerages, but bigger than most of the boutiques, usually.

The brokerage I am with now, My Home Group, is a 100% brokerage. They charge a flat fee per transaction, in my market it is under $300, and a very low monthly fee, $25.

The other 100% brokerages I worked at were similar in fees and charged slightly more per month. It was either $50 or $75 per month.

Great, right?

Depending on your market, mine is between $250,000 - $400,000 price range, this is usually less than 5% of your commission. Which is awesome!

Most of these 100% brokerages started off as boutique brokerages so they have similar focus on the marketing and technology. The difference is you must pay for the extras, like websites and CRM, yourself, usually at a better rate than getting it on your own, because they worked some type of deal out for their agents in advance.

Still sounds amazing, right? I agree!

Because of these things they will attract a ton of the local, experienced, talented agents and teams. My Home Group here in Arizona has 3 of the top 5 teams in the state, if not the top 3.

So, you have all of these "Heavy Hitters" under one brokerage and they leverage the knowledge in weekly meetings run by the agents and team leads, as well as monthly Mastermind meetings.

Most Brokerages have a closed Facebook group or business page for the agents nowadays. The one with My Home Group is like the CNN of real estate related news! 24/7 and 365 questions are being asked and answered. I can't say all 100% Brokerages are this active with their groups, but I believe the fact that these agents are keeping more of their money makes them happier and more willing to share.

But, I need to be honest and admit, that there are times you will slip through the cracks and an email or post won't get answered. At least, not as quickly as you would like.

This is, in my experience, the downside to the 100% Brokerages. Since they are growing so quickly, they may not be ready to give you the attention you need due to not having some key positions properly staffed. A similar issue to what the big name brokerage has.

What I have found is that most 100% Brokerages have big aspirations! They have towering goals! They have agents flooding to them! And, they have the growing pains that come with this.

In my opinion, this is a great problem to have, depending on the leadership.

So, this brings me to the last on the list of brokerage types for you to choose from

Tech or Virtual Brokerages – these are the newest kids on the block. They are in the mold of the Boutiques. They are quickly growing in the industry. They all have a unique "Perk" for joining them sometimes in the form of "Ownership" in the brokerage.

And, they may not be the best fit for a new agent.

I need to admit, that I know a little bit about one of the quickest growing Tech/Virtual brokerages because their agents are always excited when they join. I will tell you what I know so you can make your own decision and keep to myself what I think about them, unless you ask, nicely.

EXP Realty has agents flocking to them right now because they offer "multiple revenue streams" for their agents. They do this in a few different ways, including lead sharing and a program that reminds me of the MLM or Network Marketing business model.

They allow you to make a monthly residual income on any agents you refer to the company and joins. They also let agents donate leads you may not have gotten to, or, cannot reach and if another agent is able to work with them you get a percentage of that as well.

The idea is that agents prefer to work from home. They don't want to come in to an office to make calls. They will attend a webinar over an in-office meeting or training. Most brokerages have adapted to this and offer meeting through zoom or on Facebook live now.

With our phones, tablets and laptops handling so many of our responsibilities I can understand the draw. All the apps, software, websites and the integration with them today, it's no surprise agents are intrigued with the shiny new thing in brokerages.

I always tell my clients that us agents have a ton of great toys, when they work.

Since I have no personal experience with any of these and most of the offices are "Virtual" or "Cloud Based" I can't really speak to the quality of attention the agents receive from the virtual brokers. But I do have a few friends who can't stop telling me about how amazing it is! But I do not hear them talking about actual real estate business, transactions or closings. And, that sounds like a dig, but it is just an honest observation.

I have never done a single transaction with an agent from one of these brokerages. And, I have done over 200 transactions by myself.

Sorry!

I think I made that point.

Since I started writing this book I have been approached by 2 different Brokerages, both offering Salary, all yearly fees paid for, health benefits and more that make it feel like a corporate setting. If this interests you I am sure you will see more of them soon. I will tell you that one was Redfin, in case you've decided already this is what you want. I can't remember the other one because the person who called was rude to me on the phone.

I personally prefer getting paid commission and having control of my own finances. But that's me! And, I want you to do what feels best for you.

So, those are your options for Brokerage types. All have positives and negatives. It really comes down to you as an individual and what you feel is the best path forward.

What do you feel you need?

What do you think will help you to get to where you want to be?

Remember, I strongly suggest going with your gut feeling on this decision. You will have to do some soul searching and trust yourself. If it doesn't feel like a good fit, do not ignore that! No matter what the commission split, or fees are. Remember, I was giving away 50% of my business for my first 2 ½ years, I used that time to build my business to what it is today, a business of repeat clients and referrals.

Maybe there is a great team you can join that will give you the experience you need. That's what I did! It may not matter to you what type of brokerage they're at.

Maybe there is a specific coach, mentor or agent that you want to work with. As long as it's what you want, then go for it!

If you are moving towards your goals and hitting your targets, then, that's all that matters.

Something that is overlooked in this decision is the "partners" the brokerage has. What lender do they recommend? What Title company they use? The preferred Home Inspector? And, Home Warranty company?

In this business, one bad referral can cost you future business. It really is about who you know. Your clients are depending on you to help them with these decisions. The experience they have with the people you refer them to will have a direct affect on their impression of you.

Find out how long these partnerships have been in place. What is the benefit for you and your clients with these partners? What do the other agents think about these partners?

Often it comes down to the individuals more than the company itself. You might have the most reputable Mortgage company and get stuck with the worst loan officer, or team. The same with the Title company, it comes down to the rep you will be working with. I suggest, once you decide on the brokerage, take the time to go and meet with them. They often will have put together a list of things they can offer you to get your business going. They have apps you can forward your clients to fil out for the mortgage or find out what the closing costs will be for the home they want to buy.

The Brokers might be surprised you are asking them about the partners. The way they answer these questions should be more of an indicator than the actual answers they give you. Most Brokerages will have a list of "Vendors", which is the same thing as a partner. You want to have the conversation about who they recommend and why, not just receive a list.

You also want to ask about what the broker is going to provide. Are they making business cards or signs for you? And, how many? Is there a website? CRM? Lead genera ting? How do these change your arrangements with them?

I think you're ready to go interview Brokers. Remember, they are not interviewing you. You are interviewing them! You'll decide where you want to hang your license! None of them will say "No", so don't feel too good about the fluff they throw your way.

Trust your Gut!!! And make a decision that feels good to you!

You will make the decision official either by going back to the Department of Real Estate and making the change or going on to their website and uploading the info of who your hanging your license with there.

You will need the Brokerages License number Or ID.

Ok, now on to the next thing on our list!.... speaking of LISTS....

Third Thing: Make Your List

Yes! Make a list of everyone you know! This is the single most important thing you do as a Real Estate Agent. Without this you won't last long.

It doesn't matter what scripts you use, or how many calls you make.

It all comes down to your list.

Your list, and what you do with it, is the thing that will bring you the most success in your first year and keep you around for years to come.

Full disclosure, I did not have a list in my first year. I was still able to do 27 transactions in my first 15 months in real estate.

But, it was not easy. I was making calls all day, every day, Sunday through Saturday. I was taking calls until 11pm some nights. I was showing homes until 10pm most nights. I was out the door on Saturdays at 8am and returning at 9pm on Sunday. At least, that's what it felt like.

My Brokerage was providing internet leads because I didn't have a list. My excuse for not having a list was that I didn't know anyone because I had only lived in Arizona for 4 years and most of my friends and family were still back in California.

So, I paid the price! I paid with the most precious commodity we have as human beings. I paid with, my time. And, in my opinion, time does not equal money. You can always make more money! You can't get back or make more time.

I had to take all business that came my way. I did make some friends in that first year. I also have some of my best horror stories from my first year. Mostly about the long hours and the few ungrateful clients I helped.

Remember, I was the guy who didn't do easy. And, not having a list was why I had to do it the hard way.

If you are familiar with the 80/20 rule, then you know that just as 80% of your success comes form 20% of your clients. 80% of your headaches come from 20% of your clients also. So, you need to be able to identify who is who. This will save you from spending too much time chasing bad leads or wasting your time with people who will only make you work harder than you need to.

I learned a valuable lesson not having a list and working online leads exclusively. One that you may need to learn for yourself. But, I want to feel good knowing that 20% of you will follow this advice and not have to learn the hard way.

Make a list of al of the people that you know. That includes everyone in your phone book, in your Gmail contacts and social media accounts. Your favorite barista, the chatty cashier at the grocery store, the guy in the service department when you take your car in... EVERYONE!

For the last 3 years my business has been mostly repeat clients and referrals. The last year it has been 100% repeat and referral business. I can't express enough how huge this is to my peace of mind, success and longevity in real estate.

There is a book written by Michael J Maher called 7 Levels of Communication which tells a story of how a burned-out Real Estate Agent turns his career around when he starts using techniques he learns to create a business built on repeat clients and referrals. I highly recommend reading it! I have it on audio also and listen at least once a year. I post a link to it in a later chapter for you also.

Since making my list, I have made more money and worked with people I already have a relationship with. I do not have to sell myself before performing my responsibilities for them. I do need to maintain a level of professionalism to continue receiving their business and get referrals. But, because they know who I am, and they trust I will do what is best for them. I eliminate the possibility of losing them as long as I keep performing with their best interest in mind.

Since I made my list, I don't have to worry about spending money on leads only to have to fight to keep the lead from answering the next agents call. I am not wasting time chasing leads and trying to earn their trust and convert them to a client. This can be exhausting! And wastes that most valuable commodity we have in life, TIME!

Right now, you personally know 5 people that need to buy or sell a home. Maybe they won't use you because you're new. But more than likely, they don't know you're a licensed real estate agent, yet. This will change soon!

The truth is every single person that you know, right now, knows 5 people that need to buy or sell a house. FACT! They just need to be made aware of this, by you.

Don't believe me? Then ask around. Ask your friends and family. Make a post on Facebook "Just curious, who of my friends knows someone that is looking to buy or sell a home?"

You will be surprised.

So, open an Excel Spreadsheet. In the upper Left corner type "Name".

Then next box to the right type "Number".

Then next box to the right "Email".

Then next box to the right "Address". And if you don't have their address, that's not ok.

If you don't have the address, or if you are at your 5th box type "Relationship". Here is where things get interesting. You may want to make sure no one sees this list, seriously.

After you have all the contact info, then you need to grade the relationship you have with that person. I know, this may be difficult. But it is important for you to do this and not just have a list of names. You will be glad you did!

You will use "A" for people you know think highly of you. People that trust you and appreciate you. Yes, you want to like them also, but more important is what they think about you. Because you're "A's" are the ones who you feel will refer people to you the most.

"B" is for best friends, close cousins, someone you like being around a lot and appreciate who they are. People you like being around and spending time with. They aren't an "A" because sometimes these are the ones you will need to convince you are serious about your career choice. These are not yet the raving fans that will refer clients to you immediately. But, these will eventually refer someone once they see you are doing well.

Then work your way to "C" which are associates, co workers you are cordial with, neighbors you wave "hi" to and the favorite barista or the cashier whose line you always end up in.

If you know their name put them on the list. If you do not know their name, put them on the list and make it a priority to get their name. And, if possible their email address and phone number.

Their email address is the treasure we are really looking for. In a later chapter we will go over why when we cover CRM's. Just make sure you get them on the list for now. "C's", like in school, help you pass. Maybe not the sexiest of grades, but they help to get the job done.

"D's" people who you really don't care if you ever see or speak to again. And, be honest! Your crazy uncle who can't stop talking politics, the popular kid from High School you seem to run into more than you like and the old lady in your neighborhood that thinks she can still wear bikinis while walking her dog every morning. (you do have that neighbor, right? I can't be the only one) Believe me when I tell you that identifying the people that you do not want to work with is as important as identifying those who you do.

Some will say that "D" is for Delete. Depending on the size of your list you may be afforded that luxury. In your first year, I suggest keeping the list intact, even with the "D's".

In your first year you need everyone to know what you do. The more people who know the better off you will be. Even the crazy lady in the bikini! (Yes, I am emotionally scarred from this and hope I am not alone)

I spent a ton of money when I left my first brokerage on leads because I had to leave all the info to past clients I had helped behind. I had no list! I suggest creating a spreadsheet separate from that in your CRM in case things go south.

I was spending thousands every month for leads and ads on sites like Zillow, Realtor.com, Trulia and Homes.com. So, I needed to sell one house every month just to cover my costs for the money I spent on more leads.

Luckily for me, I had become friends with some of my past clients and kept in touch with them. My clients appreciated the experience buying homes with me and became repeat clients and referral sources. So, those became "A's" on my list when I finally started mine.

So, having a list not only makes your work a little easier because you are working with people you already know, it also saves you money.

Now, what do you do with that list? Well, you write an email and you title it "A Letter from My Heart". And you send to everyone on your list.

If you do not have a service set up like MailChimp then this might take time. But, I do not suggest BCC everyone on your list with a subject line titled that way. It will defeat the purpose.

Maybe this will take you a couple of hours, or a couple of days, but it will be well worth the time spent.

In the email you are going to tell everyone that you have spent however long it took you to get your schooling and pass your real estate exams. You will include what brought you to the decision to get your license and what you hope to achieve with your new career. You mention how excited you are about your future as a real estate agent.

Make it personal and be vulnerable.

Explain to them the process of interviewing Brokers and why you chose the Broker you did. This is your chance to have them trust you and your decision making. Use your Brokers, your team lead or coach's and office's experience to your benefit.

You want to end it letting them all know how much you appreciate them. And will cherish the opportunity to work for them. How you look forward to the opportunity to help them.

My advice is to also sweeten the pot with an offer to anyone that lets you work for them. Offer to pay for the first year of their Home Warranty (typically between$400-$750). Trust me, they will appreciate that and remember it. That is the goal.

Your PS is to call text or email you to meet up for coffee or tea. You may not want to start taking people to lunch or dinner yet. You will have many opportunities to pay for meals later, as you start helping them with their rea estate needs.

We will us this list to upload into your CRM and add drip campaigns for follow up touches. More on that in a bit.

For now, send the email with the "Letter from the Heart" and follow up a couple of days later with a text to all of them, starting with the A's. Make it short and sweet.

"Hey_____, just wanted to check in with you and make sure you got the email I sent you. Let me know when you want to meet up for some coffee or tea".

Then a few days later, start making calls. Yes, starting with the "A's". Or, you could start with the "C's" as you perfect what you are going to say but get into the "A" list ASAP!!!

Always keep the calls short. You are busy and so are they. So, practice what you will say to them, which might vary according to who they are, but always end with asking for a referral.

You do not have to ask them for their business, yet. You just want to raise their awareness and activate their radar for who in their sphere is looking to buy or sell soon.

Try something like this, and adjust the verbiage as you need to so that you always true to who you are.

"Hey Uncle Jack, I know you are busy, so I will keep it brief. I am not sure if you saw my email, but I recently got my Real Estate License and joined this amazing Brokerage. The Owner has set me up with a great Team, or Mentor, which has me really excited about my future in real estate. I just wanted to see if you maybe have talked to anyone recently that is looking to buy or sell a home that I could help? I promise to take care of them like if they are family Uncle Jack! Thank you!"

In and out, quickly. If he starts engaging, you answer his questions and keep the answers brief with the focus on the brokerage and the mentors around you.

Again, there is more to do with the list, like uploading it to your CRM and setting up your drip campaigns like I mentioned. I promise we will get to that in a bit. Just start your list immediately and remember to keep adding on to it.

Your goal is to add on to the list weekly, if not daily. The new Barista, the server at dinner the other night, your new "friends" on Facebook. Add everyone to the list, even if you do not get their email and phone number.

Without your list you will have a career of internet leads and cold calls. There's nothing wrong with that, if that's your thing! But, in my opinion, real career success and security comes from a steady stream of repeat and referrals.

So, now on to the next on our list!

Fourth Thing: Socialize

The good news is that you, like so many of us, already have most of the next step done. If not, it isn't hard to do.

The next step is fun, but it is also dangerous.

The next thing on the list is to socialize… on Social Media!

Obviously, you will need different social media accounts, and most of us already have the "must have's" in social media for real estate agents.

If you do not already, I suggest you create accounts for Facebook, Twitter, Instagram, LinkedIn and Snapchat. As of the writing of this book these are the essentials. If you are going to leave one off, I would suggest Snapchat, though if you use it correctly, that could be your strongest platform.

Be sure to use your real name on all platforms!!! If you have a popular name, make sure the variation you use is all the same among them all. For example, I am Adriel Roman and use @AdrielRoman11. I even named my website this AdrielRoman11.com.

Say what you will, but Facebook is still king when it comes to exposure and being able to keep in contact with friends, family or a broad audience.

More than 2 Billion users and growing!

Now tell me why you wouldn't want the opportunity to be where this many people are? I will wait.

Why we are still limited to only 5,000 friends on a personal account? Is another question entirely. But, they do offer Business pages and Fan pages to make up for the low contact limit on a personal account. And, I think this adds a nice layer between you and the audience this way.

With your personal page you want people to know who you are. So, you post content that tells them who you are along with pictures and anything that let's others relate to you. Then, on your business page, you stick to mostly real estate specific posts, like listings, open houses and local news.

LinkedIn will help you reach a more professional audience, in that you won't get the same type of engagement, but if you do then it will usually be a solid individual on the other end. Stick with real estate related content on this platform. I will usually post most of the same content that I do from my Facebook business page.

Yes, there still are some knuckleheads on LinkedIn, but not nearly on the same scale as on the other platforms.

I personally like Instagram the best! Though I haven't had the same level of success with actual client interactions. But, depending on the audience you attract, they seem to be more upbeat and overall nicer on IG. This platform is a visual platform, so, your best bet is to keep posts visually stimulating and upbeat, or funny. Videos uploads are less than a minute long, unless you are on IGTV, so keep your messages short, obviously.

I don't usually waste too much time with following popular celebrities, though I do follow a couple. And, I do not engage in conversations in feeds that are politically charged, which is why social media has such a bad reputation.

Which brings me to Twitter. This one is the one you really need to be selective with who you follow.

Luckily, as Realtors, we are not supposed to engage in conversations about religion or politics. Unfortunately, too many agents forget this part, especially the politics part!

Do yourself a favor, go old school with your political and spiritual views! Keep that as a personal and sacred thing. Engaging in these posts are the quickest way for you to lose an audience.

So, what do you do with your accounts? Well, you make sure your info is up to date including your new career, the brokerage you just chose and all your contact info.

Once, you have the new brokerage info updated, you share it with everyone on a post, on ALL SITES!!! And, Add a photo of you in front of the office or with the Broker, or someone attractive in the office.

"So excited to join this amazing team at _____! With all of their experience and guidance here I'm ready to help you with buying and selling your home!"

Then a couple of days later...

"How can I help you with your real estate needs?"

And, a few days later…

"Who do you know that is looking to buy or sell a home?"

Then, leave it alone for a bit.

Hopefully you are still putting up the pics of your food, your cat and the funny memes. You can't go full Real Estate Agent Professional on your audience overnight. They won't believe you and you will lose them.

Though I disagree with the consensus that us "changing" or "acting different" is a bad thing, I think it is not something that happens immediately.

As you grow professionally and hopefully personally, you want to take your audience on that journey with you. They will enjoy it, respect you and believe you if they are witnessing it in action.

You want to add photos of homes you are showing. Make videos of you walking up to the front door of a home. When you are done showing, make a video about how much you enjoyed that client, but don't mention names or go into too many details about the homes you saw.

You can mention that "house number 3 was my favorite" and give your reasons why.

During the actual transaction you may want to stay away from updates until you have the clear to close from the lender and know that documents are on their way to title. Try to get your clients to take the picture in front of their new home with key in hand. Especially in your first few transactions. Document your proof!

The down side to social media is that for so many of us it is so easy to get swept away with the noise and distractions. But, if you are interacting with real friends who can potentially become clients or referral sources, then enjoy it.

Just try to keep the comments to upbeat and positive things. Being silly is a plus! Remember to sprinkle in some info on current real estate and mortgage trends.

On Facebook, I suggest putting up the informative posts and the posts about showings and open houses on your business page. Then share it to your personal page. Identifying to everyone that there is a separation between your career and personal life.

You want to use the platforms like they are supposed to be used. So, information on the market can go on FB, Twitter and LinkedIn. Family pictures on FB and IG. If you found a cool article, depending on the content, FB LinkedIn and Twitter.

And remember to be social! Not critical! You don't want to be that person.

You can always boost posts and run ads but let's hold off on these for now. First lets just get your name and decision to start a new career path out there. Plus, we have more work to do in getting you the right exposure.

This leads us into the next thing you need to do

Fifth Thing: Get Where You Can Be Seen

Your social media and list are going to help you in creating a successful real estate career. Those are free of costs besides the sweat equity, or if you do move on to running ads and boosts. We are on social media to stay in touch with our current network of friends and family.

Because you want to maximize your exposure and the internet is still a virtual web you need to be where others are looking for people that provide the service that you are offering. You need to go to where the eyes are!

This means getting your picture and profile up on to the most popular sites for real estate searches Zillow, Realtor, Trulia and Homes.com. It is easy and free to get your information up.

Be warned, they will try to get you to spend money on advertising with them. You will have to decide on if this makes sense for your business. Regardless, you need to have yourself positioned on here with all the rest of the agents.

Good news is that since Zillow and Trulia are essentially the same company, you will only have to set your info up once, hopefully. You want to make sure that hasn't changed by checking them both. Zillow changes the way they operate more than any company I know.

Besides the exposure, the best thing about being on these sites is that you can contribute to questions asked by potential home buyers or sellers. Also, you can have clients give you reviews, and you can also share your past home sales.

I still open my Zillow profile up at Listing presentations and share my numbers for the last 12 months, what homes I sold for a buyer and which were for sellers, and what past clients are saying about my service. People know Zillow, so I use it to leverage their brand name and validate what I can provide them.

Please, please, please update your photos every couple of years! There is nothing worse in this business than a real estate agent who uses fudged photos! Whether it's a listing or your headshots, you must "keep it real" with your photos.

This part of things won't take too long. I place this after the social media section to maximize on time since you'll already be at your computer, tablet or laptop. Remember to include the links to your social media sites when you are creating your profile.

I personally believe that you will need to say something that is going to differentiate you from the rest of the agents in the "About you" sections. Don't be afraid to be colorful and show confidence since you won't be able to use the "Expert" "Guru" or "Specialist" labels too many agents use.

You can choose to write something different in each site or just copy and paste the same story. I do not think it makes a difference. I have the same thing on all my sites. I think most people are brand loyal, so if they're on Zillow, they will stay on Zillow.

It also doesn't hurt to stay on message in case they do see your info on different sites. Hopefully they remember something you said if they don't remember your photo.

I currently am trying a different approach to my Bio. Where I usually went in the same direction as most agents and tried to appear as professional as possible, now I am talking about how I will "bust my butt" working for them and go into details about what I offer that's different to other agents.

I am not advertising on these sites anymore, so I care less about how I appear because I work strictly by repeat and referral. I have occasionally gotten calls from someone off one of these sites who noticed my profile. One recently was an investor who loved the character and now we are buying and selling about 8 homes a year together.

My point is that when you are true to yourself and people believe you're being honest things end up working out for you. Often better than you expected! There I go on that Law of Attraction stuff again!

I have not paid any of these sites in over 3 years now. As I have said repeatedly, I work strictly from repeat clients and referrals. But, I do still run ads. I need to! You will need to also in this business. Ads for listings and open houses are most of my ad spend these days. I might use my Zillow Link to the listing to advertise the new listing or open house on Facebook. Or, something like that.

This will lead us into the next thing we will need to do. The next couple of things will require us to make some more choices. But these things can be optional in your first year in real estate.

Sixth Thing: Sites and CRM

In my first year as a real estate agent I did not have a personal website or a blog. The site that my Broker provided was an IDX and lead generation site. He tried a few different CRM's or Customer Relations Management systems. All he was focused on is pumping out leads and having us work them.

It worked. I was able to do 27 sales in 15 months. All off the leads I received, he generated online.

Today, we have the options of Lead Generating websites, Personal sites or Blogs and IDX sites. Most offer some sort of CRM with either preset email campaigns or you will need to create them yourself. There are even free CRM systems available.

There are some systems out there that will let you combine all elements above, or you can build what you want, which can get expensive, quickly!

In your first year I will suggest trying to keep your expenses down as much as possible. That's why I do not recommend running ads on the sites like Zillow and Realtor.com. It is also why when you're deciding on who to hang your license with you should ask about what they are providing you.

One of the 100% commission Brokerages I went to offered what looked like a nice website with CRM. Problem was that it did not work! At least, not the way I expected it to. Any time I used the site in my marketing I would not get any notifications on any new leads that came in. Instead, my leads went into the "Round Robbin" pool and distributed to other agents in the company.

Yeah, that sucked! Especially since I did not figure it out for over a month. Then, I had no way of being able to prove this was happening. Until, I uploaded a new client and she was called by an agent in a total other office.

By then the damage was done and the money was spent!

So, what is the best thing for a new agent like yourself? My answer is, "I don't know?" There really is no one solution for everyone. But the options are plentiful.

I am going to break up the websites in 3 groups, Lead Generation, IDX and Blog sites. Most Lead Generation sites do include an IDX, or, Internal Data Exchange, which is how you show the listings that are in your area, but there are significant differences.

IDX – Internal Data Exchange sites will allow your clients to view the homes that are currently on the market or on the MLS. They will also allow your clients to customize a search.

In my first year, I didn't have a need for this. My Broker was providing me with leads off his ad campaigns. Once I was in contact with someone and actively searching for homes with them, I sent them leads from my MLS. This is where most of the IDX's get their info from, but without the delay in updating.

Today, I still use my MLS to send my clients listings, even though I have my own IDX site I sign them up on. The MLS isn't fancy, in fact, it's bland, but it is up to date, so you can trust the info they are receiving.

It's a nice tool to have on your site if you do not want your clients on the other sites anymore for risk of them clicking on an agent's info and having that agent call your clients. (Which, by the way, is another great reason to work by referral only)

Blog Sites – also known as Personal Sites are the best way to develop your personal brand. Personal branding is huge in any career, especially in real estate.

Personal sites will allow your audience to get to know you more on a personal level while also delivering important information. The trick is to find the perfect balance. Too many agents are out there trying to master content, which is vital, but forget that we are the business and not the information we are providing.

What I mean is that if you answer a question, then you have done your part and provided a service. But, if you are engaging and interesting you will get people to return to you, even after you have answered the question.

You might be thinking, well, isn't that what social media is for. And, you would be correct! But, the internet is a web and you want enough platforms out there pointing in your direction as possible.

Plus, what if the social media platform that you are using is no longer relevant? What then? Well, at least you still have your Blog. The internet isn't going anywhere.

Many of us have stayed away from Blog sites because originally this was known as a site that the only way to provide content was with the written word. Now, Vlog sites, video blogs, like YouTube, allow us to post video content making it easier for us who are more comfortable this way.

Personally, I believe that using both video and writing is the most effective use of your site. I also believe that you should stay true to who you are and what you are comfortable with. If that means writing, then write away! If you are more comfortable on video, then have at it!

If you choose to mix it up, then try a 70/30 mix of personal to business posts. Again, the reason for these are to sell you, the

Brand, personally, first, then what you are providing, as a real estate agent.

You will use your social media to point people back to your Blog site and you will have links to your social media on your Blog site. Think web!

Lead Generation Sites – Are sites used to generate leads in various ways. These are great if you want to have more control and plan to run your own ads.

Some use the landing pages, which is creating a page with specific info. This could be in the form of listings in a specific city, with no HOA and have pools. Now, people looking for these criteria will hopefully "land" on your page to search for what they want.

The idea is that they will end up signing up on your site by providing you with their contact information, so you can follow up with them and convert them into your client.

Others use squeeze pages, which is a way of "Squeezing" info from people by appealing to a specific need. Probably the most used example would be the "What's your home worth?"

Again, the goal here is to collect as much info as possible. In this example, you will at very least have the address and often time also the email address and phone number.

Some Lead Generation sites make it so you can post directly to social media from their site. Others let you write blogs for your lead source. Most of these will come equipped with a CRM and offer IDX feeds.

There are so many of these sites available now and the price can get steep, quickly. Entry price on some of the less expensive are around $300 to $500 a month, while others start at $1500.

Some of these are Commissions Inc, Kunversion, Boomtown, Real Geeks, TorchX and Chime.

My first Broker had us on Real Geek when I first started, and he had that linked to InfusionSoft as the CRM at first. When that got to expensive he then switched to FollowUp Boss. A little bit later he switched to Commissions Inc an all-in-one solution and got rid of all the above. Commissions Inc was slick, but I never got to use it correctly because of the learning curve.

When I left, the first brokerage I went to a brokerage that was using Inside Real Estate, which I was not impressed with because it wasn't user friendly. So, when I left them a couple months later, I signed up with Kunversion, which I really liked, and used them for 1 ½ years. Kunversion later merged with Inside Real Estate, so go figure. Personally, I liked their system more than Commissions Inc, but I am not sure what changes Commissions Inc has made recently. I do know that there are many very happy Commissions Inc users.

Currently I am using Chime, which is a newer kid on the block. I went with them because of the site design and the look of the search page. In my opinion, this is one of the best-looking websites out, for lead generation and IDX features.

I work by repeat and referral mostly, so I can do without some of the bells and whistles that Boomtown and Commissions Inc have. And, I can keep about $1200 a month in my pocket because of that.

I tried a few other companies briefly before finding Chime. Some which had deals with my Association, but that was a mistake! I was able to work out a deal with Chime for anyone who reads this book and wants to give them a shot. Tell them I sent ya!

Now, again, I was able to live off the leads provided by my broker in my first year, without having to invest in one of these sites for myself. I also did not make my list, like you have, right? (if you haven't started on your list then please put this book down and at least write down 25 names of people you know)

My point is, that the Lead Generation sites are awesome! They make life easy! But, if you join your Realtor Association, choose the right brokerage, start your list and set up your social media, then maybe you won't need to pay for a Lead Generation site immediately.

If you do decide to invest in one of these sites, please be sure they have a CRM with auto response emails and drip email campaigns.

CRM – Customer Relations Management is a tool you will absolutely need! There are many options here also. Luckily, you can get a good one for cheap, or maybe even for free.

This could be using Gmail and the Google calendar to manage yourself, but then you don't have the Drip email campaigns, and auto responders.

Those are pre-set emails that go out automatically. "Drips" cater to a specific client or lead type and help you to stay "top of mind". "Auto Responders" go out as soon as a lead or client performs a specific act, like signing up on your website, or asks for info on a home.

Most of the Lead Generating sites and some IDX sites will come with a basic CRM. Please be sure to ask if they have the drip campaigns. If they do, ask if they have pre-set templates that you can adjust, or if you need to create them yourself.

Having pre-set campaigns that you can customize will save you time because you don't have to create the campaign from scratch. That means figuring out how many emails in a campaign. When the first and following emails will be sent. Delivering content that is informative, yet personable. But, none of this is difficult. And, it can be fun!

You want this to be as customized to your personality as possible. In most cases this is going to be the only way people get to know who you are. Also, when you have existing clients, friends and family receiving Drips, you don't want them to think you are being out of character.

When I signed up with Kunversion I just ran whatever drip they had already set in place. There were options to use other campaigns uploaded by different users. But, I didn't bother. Until I read one when I had received a response from a lead who was confused by the email they had just received from my campaign. Embarrassing!!!

When I tried some of the sites recommended by my Association I had to get my own CRM to link to my site. I went with LionDesk which was about $25 per month. It wasn't bad at all!

I did have to create my own Drips at the time. I found it to be a great experience. I got creative and maybe a little over the top with some. But, it was me being me. I used it for a few months before signing up with [Chime](). Then I made sure to look through the pre-set campaigns in Chime and I am lucky I did.

Chime had a good structure to the Drip campaigns, meaning the spacing for when the leads received the emails was good. Not too annoying and not enough time for them to forget who I was. I did adjust the content on a couple of emails and added some to the drip with personal character, but not many. I am not sure who they found to write the content. So, I am happy I had already written campaigns and with a little tweak here and there I was ready to go in a couple of hours.

There many to choose from depending on the use you have planned for them. A Blog site will allow clients to get to know you personally and build your brand better than a Lead Generation site. But, if you need to build your pipeline having a Lead Generation site is nice to have.

Seventh Thing: Start Your Routine

I wanted to call this one "Discipline" but didn't want to scare anyone away. But in case you didn't already know, you will need discipline. So, let's start with a daily routine.

This starts with your morning routine. How do you start your day? If you are like the majority of us, your waiting for the last possible minute to get up and get ready for work. Or, do you get up with time to systematically get to all the important things you need to do before starting your work day?

What is important to me may not be important to you. But, I think that we can all agree on certain things that will benefit us all, especially in the morning. Taking care of number one, yourself, is what I believe is most important.

Morning Routine - What is it that you want to do but can't find the time to do in your day? Is it Exercise? Make a healthy breakfast? Meal Prep? Meditate? Read? Walk the dogs? Stretch? Maybe Yoga?

Anything that you want more time for in your life is available if you get up early enough. I know it isn't easy, at first, but, it is necessary, so do it! You'll be glad you did! I know I am!

There is a really good book by Hal Elrod called the Miracle Morning that he has now turned into a series and even created one specifically for Real Estate Agents. This is another book I recommend you read, soon!

The first book really helped me change my life. It transformed me from the "But, I'm not a morning person" to now getting up at 7am is "sleeping in".

So, what do you do when you start waking up earlier? This is where the routine comes in. In his book he Hal has a set of suggestions for you. Things you can break up into smaller time blocks and will help you win the morning.

I recently did a 30-day program called The Kings Kit Challenge by Garrett J White and the guys from Warriorbook. They came up with their own, similar, but slightly different routine. This is when it stuck to me!

I will run through what my morning routine looks like. Again, this is something you want to cater to your own schedule. Do what feels best to you. It took me a few years to dial in my routine. This is what I am doing now. But, it may change depending on where I am in life and what I want to accomplish.

Drink Water. Now, I drink anywhere from 120 to 200 ounces of water every day. Despite the amount of water I drink throughout the day, I still wake up dehydrated. We all do! We've been without water anywhere from six to eight hours as we sleep, and our body needs to rehydrate.

I will usually start with an 8-ounce glass of water with a tablespoon of apple cider vinegar. I must warn you that the apple cider vinegar doesn't taste great, but it really does wake you up. Then, I follow that up with another 16 ounces of water by itself.

Exercise. Now, if you can, it would be great if you could get yourself to the gym first thing in the morning. But, this isn't always possible for most of us. We have kids to get ready for school and other responsibilities that may not allow us to go right to the gym first thing in the morning.

The important thing is to get moving and get the blood flowing. I personally do core workouts since it is what I skip the most when I go to the gym. You may want to run a couple of miles, or maybe take a walk. Yoga and Tai Chi are two great ways to get the blood flowing.

This might be the perfect time to walk your dogs and kill two birds with one stone. Three if you listen to an audiobook while walking. It doesn't need to be an all-out personal training session. All you really need is five to fifteen minutes to get your day off to a great start!

<u>*Meditate*</u> – There is no better time than the present! For me, this is the best part of my morning routine. A typical morning meditation for me lasts 10-20 minutes.

I personally prefer to not think about anything and just focus on my breathing. Obviously, there will be thoughts that pop into my head. When they do, I just try not to get lost in them and instead get back to focusing on my breath.

There are various techniques available. After getting into a good rhythm with your practice, maybe after two to three weeks, you can start looking into Guided Meditations, Transcendental Meditations, or any other one you feel will benefit you the most.

I use YouTube to find guided meditations or meditation music and binaural beats to meditate to. There are also some good apps like [Calm](), [Headspace]() and 1,000 Guided Meditations.

Read- For me, because I have two young boys, early morning or after 8pm, when they've been put to bed, is the only time I have available to read.

While my evening reading can be anything from sports articles, learning something I can use in my business or the latest in crypto currency news, I typically try to read something more uplifting, positive or inspiring in the morning.

For me, the goal is to get myself in an optimum state. So, reading the news or checking what's happening on my Twitter or Facebook feed first-thing in the morning is a no-no. I am trying to set the tone of the day and not be reacting to it.

<u>Write</u> – This is something I recently added to my morning routine, and I split it into two parts, Gratitude and Creating.

Gratitude is exactly what is sounds like. I spend time writing what I am grateful for from the previous day. I try to at least write five things, and the first two are usually "another day of life" and "a good night's sleep".

Some days, I can fill the page and it feels like I am not in control of myself as I write.

Other days, I struggle to get anything on the page. So, I get creative! If I do not write physical things I possess, then I write about body functions, or the weather, things we may take for granted usually.

But I always try to get at least 5 things down.

The Creating part is like a written visualization. Try visualizing the day, or something you really want to happen. There is no limit to how much you write about. And, if you prefer, then paint a very specific description of the day.

I usually try to keep this exercise to five minutes, so I set an alarm when I start. I can get very carried away at times. Also, this could be substituted for a closed eyes visualization instead. If you're artistic, you can draw a picture of something you want, or, something that makes you happy.

As you have probably realized I haven't spent any time yet checking my phone, or email. There will be enough time throughout our day to waste our time with email, social media, catching up on last nights scores and anything else that distracts you.

Try to keep the morning as your sacred space. The time to dedicate to yourself because you are worth it! Because without this time then you will default to your normal habits which probably consist of playing catch up all day, then complaining that there aren't enough hours in the day.

Time Blocking – When I was introduced to the idea of time blocking, which is blocking the time on my calendar, I though only about my work-related tasks like making follow up call.

Though these things may be important for your business, where do they fall in the "Big Picture" of your life?

I was very fortunate to take Darren Hardy's Insane Productivity course once with my first brokerage. In this awesome course he goes into creating your calendar but instead of starting with your work, starting with time blocking your personal and family plans. When a few years later I took the Peak Producer course he went through the same protocol.

Basically, you start with what is really important in life, like, birthdays, anniversaries, holidays, your kid's games, date nights with your spouse or significant other and vacations. Those become unbreakable commitments.

Then, you start filling in things like your morning routine, the time you go to the gym, days you're home for dinner and anything else that you want to keep consistent in your life.

Once you have these things dialed in, then you start filling in the time of the day you spend making your calls, working on your marketing, responding to emails, continuing education classes, work meetings and times to show homes.

Here is the secret to time blocking, this is only a template of what your schedule should look like. Besides the very first things you put on the list, the important stuff, the rest can be changed and updated. Some may disagree with me about this, but, really, if you aren't continuously making changes to your calendar, I am not sure what you are doing in life. As we grow our business and develop better routines the things we time block will change.

Plan your work around your life! Not the other way around. You may need to make adjustments to your schedule occasionally, and that is ok. If you continue to prioritize your calendar according to the things that really hold value to you, you will see that the events in your life will begin to unfold that same way.

For example, and brokers out there will hate me for saying this, I do not time block for making calls anymore. Because I am not purchasing online leads, I do not have to set the time aside to make the follow up calls. When I was new in the business and did not have my list, I made calls from 8am until 9:30 am daily, then again from 4:30pm until 6pm and a couple nights a week from 8pm until 9pm. That's what I time blocked on my calendar.

Now, I time block my calendar for spending more time doing very different things like, having lunch or coffee with past clients. I am time blocking time to post relevant content on social media. I am blocking the time I spend meeting with my lenders, title company and inspectors I work with.

Review your calendar and update it often, like you should be doing with your plans and goals in real estate. Keep adding to it, hopefully more time with your loved ones.

Nighttime Prep – I won't spend too much time on this one because it's exactly what it sounds like. And, you do not need to spend too much time on your nighttime prep either.

Quickly review your calendar for what you have on the schedule the next day. Hopefully, there are some things that are a normal part of your routine, like heading to the gym. So, you make sure you have your gym clothes and bag, if you take one, are ready for the next day.

If you have showings or other tings that you need to prepare for, then get those lined up also. Like making sure your Supra Key is charged, your laptop and/or tablet is charged, and you have your route already in your GPS so you're not dialing it in as you go.

Getting your clothes ready for the next day is not a bad idea also. It eliminates one more decision you need to make that following day. And, hopefully allows for you to have a good night's sleep.

Your routines and how disciplined you are will go a long way as a real estate agent. Your clients will appreciate it and you will save yourself from a lot of unnecessary stress. There are enough things in this business that will allow for you to be "off the cuff" and responsive.

As the saying goes "luck favors the prepared" so why not hedge your bet with discipline and time blocking what's important to you. Why not have yourself set up to succeed.

Eight Thing: Take Classes

We have a huge responsibility to our clients when we are real estate agents. We owe it to them to know the various neighborhoods they are looking at purchasing a home in. We need to understand what the mortgage industry is experiencing and what programs are available for them. We need to be able to communicate with our clients clearly, so they understand the procedure and timeline with purchasing and selling a home.

We often need to listen to our clients as they share some very personal details about their lives. We work into the late night sometimes and are available early in the morning. We are looked to provide recommendations on inspectors, painters, landscapers, and sometimes attorneys.

Because of this we need to know how to navigate through these questions and have the ability and mental fortitude to not be negatively impacted by the situations we are put in. Our clients are depending on us in one of the most important times in their lives.

We better be able to bring our A game every single day! This means not only knowing our stuff but also being able to perform at our best. Physically and mentally!

CE- Every state has very different rules about how many Continuing Education credits you need, but I think they're all due every 2 years. Where I am we need 24 credits every 2 years.

What I did when I got licensed was take as many classes as I could to get those out of the way as quickly as possible. I didn't want to worry about them later. I went over to the local association and took classes for free. Other agents thought it was a waste of time to do that because I could have paid for classes and taken them online.

But, what I didn't expect was that when I was in this room filled with 100 – 200 other agents, often more experienced than I was, I was able to learn from the quality of the questions they asked. I was new, so I had no way of applying or understanding what I was being taught. Yet time and time again the other agents would have questions which would allow the discussion to go deeper into the significance for us and how to apply these lessons.

Today I still go into my local Association for the CE classes because of this. And, I still feel like I learn so much more this way.

Often Title Agencies and Lenders will also hold CE classes and you can pay $20 and have lunch included. These are good also. In my experience there aren't as many agents that show up and often they are eating at the same time, so the level of engagement isn't the same. So, I haven't benefitted the same with these as with the one's put on by my local association.

Personal Development – "If you are not growing then you're dying!" I am not sure who came up with this quote first. But, I do remember hearing it from Tony Robbins first. This quote shook me to my core. What a concept! Which, if you think about it, then you'll have to agree with it. This is life!

Tony Robbins is one of, or maybe even the most well known in the personal development space today. Before him it was Jim Rohn. Tony and Darren Hardy both credit Jim Rohn for being their mentor, though neither one personally was mentored by Jim. They both attended Jim Rohn seminars and were immediately changed by the messages.

I recommend going out to personal development seminars as often as you can. Most of these guys have various home or online seminars available for you. At the very least, read the books they write and study them like if you are in one of the seminars.

I had one of the most memorable experiences at a [Brendon Burchard](#) High Performance Academy seminars recently. Brendon lead the four-day event, by himself. The energy was infectious, the message was impactful and best of all was getting to watch Brendon dance around on stage for 4 days. No, really! It is one of the most adorable things you will see. LOL!

The people you meet at these events can often provide as much inspiration and insight as the speakers themselves. I have made a few good friends at these events and I am sure I will see many again soon doing some big things.

Real Estate Training – When I signed up with my first broker he had us start with the [Craig Proctor](#) real estate training system. I found their script for calling on leads for the first time was one of the easiest and least intrusive ways of contacting someone for the first time. My style has always been to come from a place of service rather than sales and feel that approach is even more effective when building rapport with online leads.

My first broker was really into training and so next we did the [Dirk Zeller](#) Real Estate Champions training. Personally, this wasn't my favorite training. But, the rest in my office felt like it helped them tremendously. He went into a variety of scripts for different situations, which is great. He also pushed us for developing and sticking to our schedule.

I just felt it was too much on the sales side for me and that his scripts were preying on people's fears. Also, he gave me a hard time because I made a less calls that the others in my office made, even though I was getting more appointments and contracts.

Then we did the [Brian Buffini](#) Peak Producer training. This was were it really started to get fun for me. This whole system is based on getting your business to the point where you are working by referrals only. It was so great, in my opinion, that I went through this training 4 more times and got certified to train this system.

There are plenty of real estate coaching sites out from [Mike Ferry](#) to one from an agent in my brokerage [Joshua Smith](#). There are various styles and price ranges for training to choose from. My recommendation is to peruse the sites and click on the free content they offer to find out who's style resonates the most with you. Who is going to get you to where you want to be. And, sometimes you'll need to do a few different ones then pick bits of pieces of each and make them your own.

Personal Training and Gym classes – I apologize! I haven't spent nearly enough time on the subject of physical wellness and how important it is for real estate agents.

No, this isn't a physically demanding profession compared to many other jobs out there. You may spend most of your time sitting in a car, and not much physical activity at all most of your day. And, this is exactly the reason why making the time to exercise is so important!

It was early December of 2016 and I was pulling up to a listing appointments home. I had been dealing with a nagging pain down my left leg. I would usually spend all of about 10 seconds stretching half-heartedly to try and alleviate the pain, then try to mentally block out the pain. This time, the pain was so intense I almost fell to the ground. My hamstring felt as if it was going to snap. After about 2 or 3 minutes of stretching, talking to myself and trying to walk it off, I was able to enter the home and give my presentation.

The next day I was driving around showing houses when it happened again. This time right in front of my clients. Luckily, I had worked with them before, so they didn't judge me, too much. But, it was the most painful and embarrassing experience.

Until the next week, when getting out of my car to show another house, to the same clients, I ripped my pants so badly, I had to use my bag to cover myself.

I had gone to my doctor the previous week when the pain got nearly knocked me to the ground. After all the bloodwork and series of tests including not being able to touch my toes, he told me that I was too heavy and was practically borderline diabetic. I am 5'10" and was used to walking around at about 175 lbs to 180 lbs. I had gained about 25 lbs since becoming a real estate agent and since we were right in the middle of the holiday season, gaining another 5 – 10 pounds would be no problem. And, so I waited until after the holidays, and after gaining another 7 lbs, to start my New Year resolution to go on a diet.

It was great! I lost 25 lbs in 30 days doing the Whole 30 Paleo diet! Then, at the end of February of 2017, I had already put 15 lbs back on. And, there was the sciatic pain that shot down my leg again.

So, I decided to join a local gym and hire a personal trainer. After my initial consultation and letting them know what my issues were and what I wanted to accomplish, they set me up with this body building ex-Marine.

I was worried, thinking I had made a big mistake and tried to find any way out of making my appointments. He had seen it and heard it all, so he didn't let me off the hook. Plus, I had already paid for the sessions in advance, and wasn't going to get my money back. After letting my trainer know what my biggest concern was, he got me on a program that within 2 months, had me looking and feeling amazing. And, I haven't stopped going to the gym since!

I have been with 3 trainers in the last 2 years. I attend group classes to break the monotonous routines we can easily fall in when going to the gym to lift. I even include some Yoga classes, which are more challenging, and rewarding, than I ever imagined!

What I have been through in the last couple of years, with the transformation to my business, my commitment to learning and improving, along with the physical energy to perform have been what I can only describe as magical!

My mood is better! I sleep better! I wake up every morning before 5am and feel great! I still eat a lot, and, I am working on my diet, but that's a subject for another book. My point is, being healthy, exercising comes with so many unexpected benefits, I really think it is something we must add to our routine. For our own well-being, for the well-being of our family and for our clients.

Ninth Thing: Read Lots of Books & Listen to Audio Books

Staying up to date with what is happening in our industry is essential. This is why I put the previous chapter on continuing education before this one. I believe that as real estate agents we must continue to learn and grow in order to become the person who attracts the types of clients we want to work with. In my opinion, personal development is the most important aspect of being an agent. The development of one's person and character will contribute directly to the types of clients you work with and your longevity in real estate. It is also one of the least talked about aspects, even though there is always a large amount of real estate agents at personal development seminars.

As I suggest taking as many classes as you can in your first few months in the previous chapter, I will suggest reading as much as you can and continuing with the habit as a lifestyle. Reading books is less expensive than attending classes or seminars and sometimes just as effective, if not more. I have a pen and pad with me and take notes as I read, like I would do in a class or seminar.

Recently I've been hearing about the "[5 Hour Rule](#)" that Bill Gates, Warren Buffett and other successful people are committed to. Basically, they spend 5 hours a week reading or learning something new. If it is good enough for them, then it should be good enough for us! This is why I recommend continuing education classes, seminars, AND reading 5 hours a week.

How much time should we devote to reading? Well, there are a few different ideas on how much time we should spend reading. I believe that most will say it would be best if you spent an hour reading every day. In my opinion we should spend at the very least 30 minutes a day, every day, reading. Like Jim Rohn says, "miss a meal, but don't miss your time to read".

Others say to read 10 pages a day. With reading 10 pages daily, you will have read 3,650 pages in a year. Which is the equivalent of twelve three hundred-page books. Which is not bad!

Obviously, if you're going to spend time reading, read what makes you happy! Read novels, biographies, fiction and sci-fi.

You can never read too much. Just remember to add a few books in the personal development category also.

Personal development has a huge variety of sub topics to choose from. You can read books about morning routines, how to increase productivity, marketing, improving your memory, mindset, negotiating, diets, and different ways to exercise.

Ok, I understand that maybe you feel like you do not have the time to sit and read as much as recommended. But, we all have time to listen to an audiobook. You can easily listen as you commute to and from appointments and showings. While walking your dogs, doing dishes, cooking dinner or doing the laundry. Take every opportunity possible to fill your head with knowledge or at least something inspiring.

I prefer to listen to a good book while at the gym over listening to music. But, this means that not only does the content of the book have to be interesting, but the reader needs to have character. This is how I chose my list of recommended audio books to follow.

I included a list of books and audiobooks I recommend which have helped me considerably in my career and personal life.

These are in no particular order. Find something you might be interested in and have at it! Enjoy!

For the complete list of books I recommend visit
https://adrielroman11.com/

Recommended reading list

[Miracle Morning](#) by Hal Elrod– And, for [Real Estate Agents](#) by Hal Elrod and Michael J Maher

The Miracle Morning Series has developed into one of the most influential personal development movements of our time. I, like so many who picked the first book up, was not a morning person. I would regularly stay up until one or two in the morning, then get up after hitting snooze four or five times. Then I am running around, in a bad mood, playing catch up the rest of the day.

This book helped put the importance of getting the much needed "me time" in daily, and what better time than before everyone else is up in order to eliminate distractions. I've read about 4 in the series now, some more than once, and a couple to get me back on track when I start slacking and fall back into my old routines.

To understand the one written for real estate agents, which is written as a story, you will want to have read [Seven Levels Of Communication](#) – by Michael J Maher, which I reference in the next list on audiobooks.

[The Compound Effect](#) – by Darren Hardy

Darren Hardy, if you're not familiar with him, is the CEO of [Success Magazine](#), which has been around since the 1890's with contributors like W Clement Stone and Napoleon Hill, writer of [Think and Grow Rich](#).

This book is also on my audiobook list, because it is that great! And, it is entertaining with some awesome stories.

Make a decision and work towards it, daily! Simple enough, right! And, also simple enough not to do. Darren is great at walking us through the effects of taking the appropriate actions, or not.

[The Richest Man in Babylon](#) – by George S Clason

A classic and must reads for us who want help with financial planning and personal wealth.

1. Start thy purse to fattening
2. Control thy expenditures
3. Make thy gold multiply
4. Guard thy treasure from loss
5. Make of thy treasure a profitable investment
6. Insure a future income
7. Increase thy ability to earn

Money and riches are in abundance for those who can master the rules of acquiring it.

Secrets of the Millionaire Mind – by T Harv Eker

After reading this book I was inspired so much that I searched online and found that there was a Millionaire Mind Intensive, which is a three day seminar, in Phoenix 2 weeks later. So, I went and spent three transformational days with some amazing people.

I then signed up for one of their packages and spent the next year travelling to Los Angeles for various training seminars on topics from marketing to identifying your passion. Yes, we "High Fived" and hugged a whole lot! And, it was awesome!

The book is two parts. One, identifying your money blueprint, and, two, "Wealth Files" which explains how "The Rich" think differently then those who are not rich.

[High Performance Habits](#) – by Brendon Burchard

Like my experience reading Secrets of the Millionaire Mind, when I was done with this book, I found out that in the next couple of weeks Brendon Burchard was in Phoenix for a four-day High Performance Academy event.

Being able to piggyback the experience of the seminar after reading the book was phenomenal! Again, I made some good friends, hugged and danced around for four days as I learned and transformed myself.

The book is in divided into three sections, with six habits and how to sustain them for high performance. For me, this has been one of the easiest to understand and easily applicable personal development books I have read.

I also recommend this book in audiobook because Brendon is another charismatic guy.

[The Master Key System](#) – by Charles F Haanel

Some say that this is where Napoleon Hill got his 16 [Laws of Success](#) from, which lead to "Think and Grow Rich". Both are great to read by the way and both are classics in personal development.

My belief is that this one leans more towards the practices of the Law of Attraction. But, I also believe that they are both, personal development and law of attraction, one in the same. More on that in a later book.

I will say that since this book was written long ago it is not always the easiest to read. But, that could just be my problem.

[The Alchemist](#) – by Paulo Coehlo

This one is a classic for us that are into the Law of Attraction! A great story of how the universe conspires to your benefit once you decide on something.

This is another book I read repeatedly. Paulo Coehlo has a great writing style that just easily draws you in, paints very vivid pictures of the scenery and allows you to feel what the characters are experiencing.

Tools of Titans – by Tim Ferris

I am so grateful for Tim Ferris and the books he puts out. In this one he gives us bits and pieces from interviews with some of his guests on his podcast.

He interviews Tony Robbins, Arnold Schwarzenegger, Jocko Williink, Jamie Foxx, Rick Rubin and many more.

He divides the book into 3 parts, Healthy, Wealthy and Wise. Though many of the interviews and advice could probably transcend into other areas, the format is awesome, and the tips and advice given is awesome to have all in one place.

Own the Day – Aubrey Marcus

Aubrey Marcus is the founder and CEO of Onnit, an optimal human performance company, which has among many things, supplements and exercise equipment. He is what is considered an experimentalist, he is into unconventional fitness, and what some might call a bio hacker or human optimizer.

The premise of this book is simple. Win one day and see how you feel. Then, after that, you can decide what works for you and continue to use those tools moving forward.

From your morning routine to your sleep environment and everything in between, including the meals you eat, is covered in this book so you can own the day.

For the complete list of books I recommend you read please visit AdrielRoman11.com/recommended-reading

Recommended Audio Books

Crush It & Crushing It – by Gary V

If you are not following Gary Vaynerchuk, do yourself a favor and start now! Gary V is one of my favorites because of his character, how much he genuinely cares and his candor. Because of this I prefer the audiobook. You feel the sincerity of his message that probably would not translate the same reading the pages of the book.

We are business owners and we are our personal brand. As soon as you accept that then the sooner you will work to improve your marketing and branding. The most effective and efficient ways of doing this is through social media.

Gary V has books available and he makes himself available on almost all social media platforms. These books are filled with info on how to best get yourself on the right platform to promote yourself while staying true to who you are as a person and brand.

Seven Levels Of Communication – by Michael J Maher

Michael J Maher tells the story of a struggling real estate agent that turns it around by working his list and sphere of influence.

I have read and listened to this book more than once and now make it a habit to listen to it at least once a year.

Here, in this book, is the baseline blueprint to building a business of repeat clients and referrals. This along with the Buffini Peak Producer Training is what got me to transform my business from chasing online leads to where it is today, 100% repeat clients and referrals.

Michael also writes the Miracle Morning for Real Estate Agents and continues the story line with the same agent which is awesome! These have helped me so much with my business.

Extreme Leadership & Dichotomy of Leadership - by Jocko Willink & Leif Babin

My wife teases me about this one. She says this is a "Guy's Book" because it is filled with stories by the authors about the time they spent serving In Iraq as Navy SEALS.

I think that along with the great stories on the battlefield, they do a great job of also telling stories of how to apply the lessons on leadership in our civilian situations at work.

The authors both read the book themselves and because of their awesome voices and intensity it helps to get the message across.

You Are A Badass – By Jen Sincero

No, I didn't add this one just to offset the previous book that could be mostly for guys. I really enjoyed listening to Jen Sincero read her book and her message is easy enough to understand and apply.

I believe we all need help with our mindset and often need reminders while on our journeys. This is what I got from this book. A reminder of who I am and why I do the things I am doing.

7 Strategies for Wealth & Happiness – by Jim Rohn

I can't have a list of personal development audiobooks without including one by Jim Rohn. Reading his books are good. But, listening to him speak is so much better!

His message mixed with his delivery and ability to make us laugh is why so many have been positively affected by Jim Rohn. Tony Robbins and Darren Hardy both refer to Jim as their mentor, though neither one was directly taught by Jim. But, when you listen to him enough, you can't help but feel like he is talking directly at you!

The Science of Getting Rich – by Wallace D Wattles

This is another classic! I prefer it to listen to over reading because I find it easier to understand since it was written in the early 1900's and published in 1910.

I was turned on to this book after watching The Secret. This is one of the books Rhonda Byrne says introduced her to the Secret.

Wealth Can't Wait – by David Osborn

For some reason it took me reading this book then listening to this on audiobook a second time to fully appreciate this book. I had read Miracle Morning For Millionaires and I loved it which is co written by David Osborn. I then decided to give this book a second try on audiobook and loved it!

High Performance Habit – by Brendon Burchard

and

Compound Effect – Darren Hardy

These are both listed in the books to read and I added them here also because they are great in both formats.

For the complete list of books I recommend you read please visit

https://adrielroman11.com/recommended-audio-books

A Few More Things

Calls and Follow Up – for a new real estate agent there probably are not a more difficult thing to get used to than making calls to ask for business and following up with the people you have talked to. I get it! It is still one of the toughest things for me.

Unfortunately, this is one of the most important aspects of our work as real estate agents.

In my experience I was able to find the most success by coming from a customer service angle versus the sales agent. I tried to ask the right questions to get the clients more comfortable with me. Build rapport, get them to like you then it will be easier for them to trust you and work with you.

Bad clients - One of the most memorable times I had as an agent happened about 2 years in. At this point in my career I was still working off the online leads provided by my brokerage. I was mostly working with buyers and constantly on the run showing homes.

I was working with this couple who I had shown about 15 homes to and they finally put an offer in on a home they liked. Great! Except, it was about 20% lower than the asking price by the seller. I explained to them that we should probably expect a counter from the seller, which they confirmed was their expectation also. I even went into more detail and explained that because we had come in with a very low offer, we should also expect the counter to be close to the asking price. At the time it was a sellers' market and they were priced reasonably.

As expected, we received a counter and it was near the original asking price. My clients decided they would continue to look instead of responding to the counter. I was surprised because the home had checked off on all the boxes for this couple. Instead of having the conversation about expectation with them like I should have I said nothing.

I kept showing them homes, about 20 more, and they did the very same thing a couple more times, low offers at about 20%

of asking price. Both times they walked away instead of responding to the counter.

Then, we actually got someone to accept our low offer! I was excited! But, instead of celebrating the win, they ended up deciding that they didn't go low enough on the offer and that was why the sellers had accepted it. They didn't even deposit the earnest money and decided to verbally cancel instead of putting it in writing like we are supposed to do.

At this point I was upset, confused and worried I would never be able to find them a home. So, I went to speak with my broker about this.

He looked at me and without hesitation told me to "fire them". I was shocked!

I had spent weeks showing them over 40 homes. How could I walk away from them at this point? I didn't have anything else in the pipeline because I spent all my time with this couple.

My broker told me that was exactly the reason why I needed to fire them. I would never get them under contract and will kill my business if I didn't let them go immediately. He also said that it would make me feel good afterwards.

So, I did! And, he was right! I felt liberated! I felt like I could fly again! My wife even mentioned to me that she was happy I fired them because I was being very negative and not fun to be around because of those clients.

Yes, there are bad clients! This is why it is important to identify who is who on your list. It is also important to understand that the 80/20 rule works in a negative way as well. 80% of your problems will be caused by 20% of your clients.

Don't be afraid to fire your client, if there is good reason to!

Surround yourself with good people - In real estate, there is never a dull moment! You will have to learn to enjoy the experience, learn from the experiences and identify the situations when they start to feel like a similar experience from the past, both good and bad. Though no two transactions are ever the same, there are similarities in most transactions.

Being able to step back and look at your present situation objectively might not be easy. This is another reason why who you choose to hang your license with is important. I was lucky to have access to my first broker and go over the scenario with him.

Having a coach, broker or teammate to bounce ideas off is important. Thinking you can handle everything on your own is a mistake. You need to be surrounded by good people, who want you to succeed.

Save money– Hopefully, you have some money put away. Though it is possible to get something under contract and closed in your first month, more times than not, that isn't the case. This is the single biggest reason so many agents quit in their first year and return to working a nine to five.

Also, another reason agents quit or get themselves in trouble and are forced to leave the industry, is because we don't always prepare ourselves by properly budgeting our finances.

For many of us, this is the most money we have made. So, we spend every penny we receive. Then, when it is time to pay taxes at the end of the year, we are broke. Trust me, I know this story very well.

Or, we go and get the new car, which, in itself isn't a bad idea, but, do we really need the S Class??? (I was at least smart enough to start with the C Class)

There is something to be said for getting yourself in a position to work hard for what you have. Adding an incentive like a car payment does have some positive effects on us. But, not if you are not able to eat, just so you can look good!

Invest in yourself - I touched on this point a few times throughout the book and just want to circle around to it once again. Investing in yourself through reading and personal development courses online or live is highly encouraged. You cannot improve on yourself too much!

More than any technology, investing in yourself is the best and wisest investment you can make. It yields the highest returns. You can take the lessons you learn and apply them in all aspects of your life, not just real estate.

Yes, it will help you grow your business. Which is great! But the effects it has on your spouse, kids, neighbors, family and friends is priceless.

Never stop learning and thriving to be better! Whatever that means for you! Because, you are the only one that knows what "Better" looks like for yourself.

LOA and attracting clients – Yes, this again. And, if this isn't for you, then fine! I am not in your shoes. I can only speak from my own experiences. And, my experience is that the more I worked on myself, the more I attracted clients I wanted to work with.

The more time I spent contemplating what I wanted my business to look like and operate like, the more these things seemed to magically happen for me.

But, I had to be clear of what I wanted. And, I had to be able to state it in the positive! Not only identify what I didn't want, but also, what I did want. Very specifically. Sometimes more generally until I was clear enough to be specific without causing too much of a contrasting feeling to develop in me.

Once I was able to clearly understand that **I wanted** my business to consist mostly of listing homes is when it happened for me. When I realized that **I wanted** my clients to come from referrals or be my past clients then that is what happened. When **I decided** that my past clients would be the only ones I would go out showing homes to it was almost magical how my business transformed.

Yes, it started with **not** wanting to work online leads and chase leads until they became clients. It started with **not** wanting to drive around all day 7 days a week showing homes. But, that just attracted more of the same.

Again, only you know what you want in your life. Learn to positively state what you want and watch how much of a difference that makes.

I was fortunate to meet so many great people as I worked online leads. That experience I would not pass up. It was great! It was fun! And, it helped me to grow a successful business. For that I am forever grateful.

But, working by referral is how I will continue to do business from here on out.

The Four Agreements - I didn't add this to my list of recommended reading and probably should have. The book [The Four Agreements](#) is another great book that I feel translates directly into our responsibilities as real estate agents. If we can live by these, at least in our work as agents, I believe you will have great success.

The Four Agreements are:

1. Be Impeccable with your Word: Speak with integrity. Do what you say and say only what you mean. Don't spend time gossiping about others. Use your words only in the direction of truth and love.

2. Don't Take Anything Personally

Nothing others do is because of you. Do not be offended by others because what others say and do is a projection of their own reality.

3. Don't Make Assumptions

Ask questions. Communicate with others as clearly as you can to avoid misunderstandings. This agreement is so important and with it you can completely transform your life.

4. Always Do Your Best

Your best is going to change from moment to moment depending on the circumstances including your health. Always do your best! And, you will avoid self-judgment, self-abuse, and regret.

I wish you much success in your career! Welcome, and remember to keep smiling!

www.ingramcontent.com/pod-product-compliance
Lightning Source LLC
Chambersburg PA
CBHW020435220526
45464CB00002B/708